North Devon
Pub Walks

Robert Hesketh

Bossiney Books · Launceston

All the walks in this book were checked prior to printing, at which
time the instructions were correct. However, changes can occur in the
countryside over which neither the author nor the publishers have any
control. Please let us know if you encounter any serious problems.

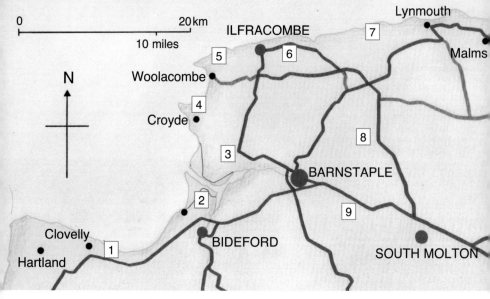

The approximate locations of the walks in this book

Some other Bossiney books you may find useful

Exmoor Pub Walks (8-15km walks)
Shortish Walks North Devon (6-8km walks)
Shortish Walks on Exmoor (6-9km walks)

Exmoor, a Shortish Guide
Lynton and Lynmouth, a Shortish Guide
Devon's Geology

For a full list of Bossiney books, please see our website.

First published 2009 by
Bossiney Books Ltd, Langore, Launceston, Cornwall PL15 8LD
www.bossineybooks.com

© 2009 Robert Hesketh All rights reserved
ISBN 978-1-906474-09-6

Acknowledgements
The maps are by Graham Hallowell
Cover based on a design by Heards Design Partnership
All photographs are by the author or from the publishers' own collection

Printed in Great Britain by R Booth Ltd, Penryn, Cornwall

Introduction

Most of these routes are between 8 km and 14 km (5 and 8 1/2 miles) in length, though one is 18 km (11 miles) but fairly flat. All can be walked in a day and some could be completed in a morning or an afternoon. It is best to start with the shorter walks if you are out of practice, to build your stamina. The time you need depends on how fast you walk and how interested you are in what you see.

Safety (please take seriously)

Walking in North Devon is generally safe and trouble-free – but be prepared, especially for sudden changes in the weather. Despite a generally mild climate, high winds and fogs are not unknown – not to mention rain! Good walking boots and suitable clothing, including waterproofs, are a must. So are drinking water and a comfortable rucksack. Many, including me, add a walking stick, mobile phone and food to the list. Long trousers are recommended, as a defence against nettles, briars and the ticks which can carry Lyme disease.

The relevant OS Explorer map will add to the interest of the walk, and could be useful if you do go astray or need to modify your route.

Many of the pubs are family run, so it may be advisable to check their opening times before starting your walk.

Access

Please keep to the paths over enclosed farmland, use (and close) gates as appropriate and keep dogs under control.

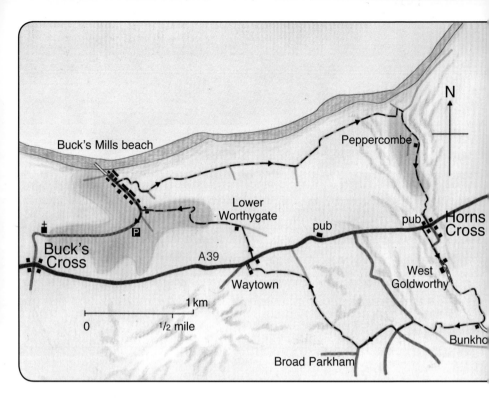

Walk 1 Buck's Mills and Horns Cross

Distance: 10km (6¼ miles)
Time: 3½ hours
Character: A mix of coast, woodland and field paths, this walk has varied scenery and excellent coastal views. The start is at Buck's Mills, once a harbour with its own quay and limekilns, but now one of the quietest and most unspoilt places on the North Devon coast. This is quite a strenuous walk, and liable to be very muddy and/or overgrown in places, so wear good boots and long trousers.

Start from the free car park at Buck's Mills – signed from Buck's Cross on the A39. Turn right and follow the lane downhill for 450m. Either turn right here on COAST PATH PEPPERCOMBE (beside a red phone box at the time of writing) or continue for a further 200m on the lane to visit the beach – especially interesting at low tide (see page 6) – then retrace your steps.

From the red phone box, take COAST PATH PEPPERCOMBE steeply up-hill through Worthygate Woods. When the path divides, keep left PEP-PERCOMBE. The path finally levels out at 132m above sea level.

Continue ahead COAST PATH PEPPERCOMBE at the next two junctions. As the path begins to descend towards Peppercombe, look out for a break in the trees on the left. This superb viewpoint reveals a great stretch of rocky shore, flanked by red cliffs with the huge curve of Bideford Bay beyond. There is also a welcome bench.

Turn right at the next path junction, GREENCLIFF, then continue up the track for HORNS CROSS. Follow the HORNS CROSS signs uphill to a tarmac drive. Turn left along it to the Coach and Horses (01237 451214), ideally situated half-way round this walk.

Cross the main road and turn right along it for 50m, then turn left about 5m before the PUBLIC FOOTPATH sign. Cross the stile ahead and follow the field edge to a concrete track. Continue ahead past West Goldworthy farm on your left, then a barn on your right, and on to a grassy track. Leave the track when it bends right. Cross a stile and follow the field edge ahead to a gate. Go through and after 20m cross the stile on the right and keep the hedge on your right to Bunkhole.

Keeping to the right of the house and then the fruit garden, walk ahead through a series of gates. Continue through a field, with the hedge on your left, but only as far as a disused field boundary, now a

low mound. Turn right and uphill. Cross the stile and turn left down a muddy enclosed track to a stream. Cross the footbridge and after 50 m turn right, PUBLIC FOOTPATH.

On reaching a lane, turn left, then right (BROAD PARKHAM) at Fox-down Cross. Climb a hill, then when the lane veers left, bear right on a track between farm buildings. When this track divides, keep left. When it divides again, bear left. Follow the track to a tarred drive, and turn right.

Turn right again onto the main road. Follow the verge for just 30 m, then turn left across a stile, PUBLIC FOOTPATH, and walk ahead towards the farm (Lower Worthygate). Follow the path to the right of the farm-house, then turn left, PUBLIC FOOTPATH. Pass the farmhouse on your left. Do not walk into the field directly ahead, but bear right up a slight slope and through a small wooden gate, PUBLIC FOOTPATH.

Cross a stile and keep the field hedge on your left. Go through a gate and follow the path downhill to Buck's Mills. Turn left up the lane to the car park.

Buck's Mills beach

The diversion involves a steep descent and ascent, but the effort is repaid with spectacular views. The dramatic rocks are folded and contorted layers of siltstone and shale, interbedded with harder sandstone. Different rates of erosion have produced the ridges. The rocks and waterfall are best seen at low tide. An information board by the beach gives details of Buck's Mills' history.

Walk 2 Bideford, Appledore and Westward Ho!

Distance: 18km (11 miles)
Time: 5 hours
Character: Boats, especially fishing and pleasure craft, keep Bideford and Appledore busy. This long but mainly level route leads past quays and boatyards and over the dunes of Northam Burrows to a vast sandy beach and the roaring Atlantic surf, then returns via quiet footpaths and lanes.

Start from the long-stay section of Bideford's riverside car park. Walk downriver, away from the medieval Long Bridge, to pass under the modern Torridge Bridge. The COAST PATH is well signed, using the

---

The Beaver Inn at Appledore 01237 474822

It probably got its name from the North America trade which made Bideford and Appledore rich during the 17th and 18th centuries. Tobacco was the most profitable element but beaver pelts and other products, including cod, also played a part. No doubt sailors returning from America celebrated at the Beaver and other riverside inns. The Beaver is also said to have been used by the local press gang, which took sailors for forced service in the Royal Navy: their officers wore hats called beavers.

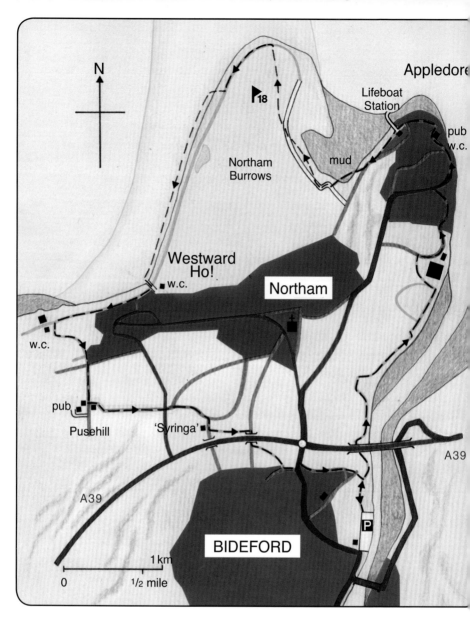

quay, footpath and occasionally quiet streets as it winds its way towards the sea. Keep your feet dry by using the signed high-tide diversions as needed.

You will in time reach a lane. Turn right, for APPLEDORE. At a T-junction with the main road, turn right to Appledore Quay, noticing the Richmond Dry Dock on your right. Walk along the Quay, through a car park and into IRSHA STREET. This leads past the Beaver and the Royal George to the Lifeboat Station.

Keep right, past the Lifeboat Station and along the COAST PATH to Northam Burrows. Again, high and low tide alternatives are marked. The inlet here is mostly mud rather than sand, so stick to the edges.

On reaching the toll hut, start by following the road north, then continue in the same direction when the road curves away. Keep well to the right of the golf course – said to be the oldest in England. Turn left on reaching the pebble ridge and simply follow it to Westward Ho! If the tide is out, walk on the hard sand.

Leave the beach via the slipway. Follow the COAST PATH along the sea wall and out of Westward Ho!, a seaside resort which was named after Charles Kingsley's swashbuckling Devon novel of 1855.

Continue past various kinds of holiday accommodation. Ignore the first PUBLIC FOOTPATH on the left, but take the second – just before public conveniences. After 100 m the path is signed KIPLING TOR.

Rudyard Kipling went to the United Services College in Westward Ho! and set his *Stalky and Co.* here – it is based on Kipling's own schooldays. Continue uphill, ignoring side turnings. Follow the path past houses. Cross a lane and enter another, which leads down to the hamlet of Pusehill.

Either take the first PUBLIC FOOTPATH left, before entering Pusehill, or – if in need of refreshment at the expense of 500 m extra walking – continue ahead through Pusehill and turn right to the Pig on the Hill – a pub serving good local beers but in an untraditional setting. Return through Pusehill to the footpath, now on your right.

Follow the footpath through fields to Silford Cross. Cross the road and walk straight ahead along the lane – do not take the left turn to NORTHAM. Keep right when the lane divides. After 100 m, opposite 'Syringa', turn left onto a footpath.

Turn right onto a lane under the A39, then immediately left onto the footpath continuation. Go through a metal gate, then keep the hedge on your right. Turn left onto a lane. Cross the main road, turning left, then right into ORCHARD HILL.

Climb the hill, then descend the other side. At CHANTERS ROAD, continue ahead on a footpath and bear right through houses. Turn left at the end of NEWBRIDGE CLOSE, then turn right to rejoin the coast path. Retrace your steps to the start.

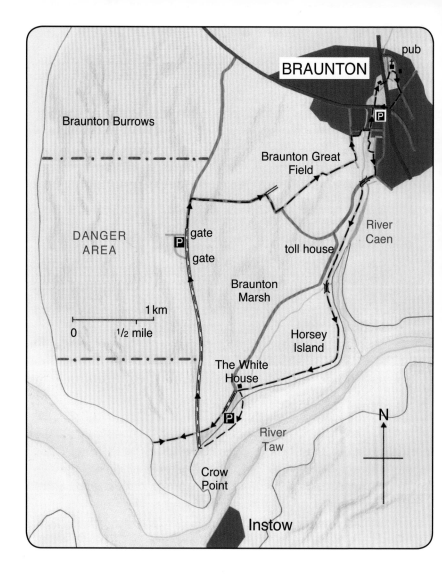

Walk 3   Braunton and the Burrows

Distance: 14.5 km (9 miles)

Time: 4 hours

Character: This level walk explores the area where the rivers Taw and Torridge meet the Atlantic in a broad estuary, flanked by massive sand dunes (Braunton Burrows) and reclaimed marshland. The return is through Braunton Great Field, a rare survival of a medieval open strip field though the number of separate strips is now greatly reduced.

Our directions start from Braunton's main car park by the Bakehouse Centre, which houses an excellent museum and Tourist Information Centre, but if you do start here, there will be no facilities during the whole route. You may prefer to start from the car park at Crow Point, at the end of the toll road, which will give you the facilities of Braunton (pub, toilets, shops) at the mid-point of the walk.

With your back to the Bakehouse Centre and facing down the car park, bear right and take the riverside path. Follow the path on through waste ground to a tarmac cycle track. Turn right along it and continue to a roundabout.

Turn right, COAST PATH TARKA TRAIL. Follow the lane over a bridge, then immediately turn left up steps and follow the riverside path past Velator Quay. Now used by pleasure craft, Velator once took ships of up to 130 tons with cargoes of coal, fertiliser and farm produce, as evocative photographs in the museum show.

Stay on the Coast Path around the perimeter of Horsey Island. At the White House, where the Appledore ferry used to land, the Coast Path is signed behind the dunes, on a rough track to the parking area. At low tide, it's pleasanter to walk along the beach, and then turn right beyond the parking area.

To see Braunton Burrows and Saunton Sands, follow the board walk ahead (i.e. turning left if you are coming inland from the beach) and over the dunes. After enjoying the views, retrace your steps along the board walk. Turn left onto a stony track, known as 'the American Road'. Stay on the track for 2.3 km and continue through metal gates and past a car park and onto tarmac, Sandy Lane.

Take the first turn right and follow it for 1.3 km past Willowfield and past the first turning left – an unsigned track. Take the PUBLIC FOOT-PATH left at a stile and metal gate. Follow the broad path all the way across Braunton Great Field. Ignore the footpath right at a stile, but continue ahead, following the path sharp left, and then into a street.

After 200 m, at MILL STILE, turn right, PUBLIC FOOTPATH. At the end of the path, turn left then right over a bridge. Turn immediately left and retrace your steps along the river bank to the Bakehouse Centre.

The Black Horse, St Brannock's church and the older part of Braunton are all well worth visiting. Leave the car park past the Bakehouse Centre and cross the road at the pedestrian lights. Take the footpath KNOWLE ILFRACOMBE. Walk past the bowls club then turn right along

The tidal mud-flats of the River Caen, just south of Velator Quay

Braunton Burrows is a UNESCO Biosphere Reserve. The Burrows host a remarkable variety of flora. Please tread carefully: some plants are endangered, some unique

a path in front of cottages. Cross the main road. Continue ahead on PUBLIC FOOTPATH to the church porch, then out to the Black Horse.

Facing the pub, turn right along Church Street. Take the first turn right, BRAUNTON. At the junction, bear half right in front of the hardware store and continue to the car park.

Military training

Braunton Burrows are used as a training area. Do not pick up metal objects or enter the area if red flags are flying – which implies live firing. At other times, the Burrows are open to the public. Don't be startled if you see soldiers or military vehicles, but keep out of their way!

The Black Horse 01271 812386

Thought to be at least 300 years old, this Grade II listed pub has a good collection of historic local photographs. It is also a venue for tug-of-war and skittles matches.

Walk 4   Croyde and Georgeham

Distance: 12.3km (7¹/₂ miles)
Time: 4 hours
Character: This beautiful route offers a variety of scenery, from surf-washed sands and rocky cliffs to flower-strewn paths and green fields. Croyde and Georgeham are noted for their thatched buildings.

Start from Croyde's village hall car park. Turn right, then left 20m ahead. After a further 40m turn right across the stream and follow Watery Lane to the top. Turn left and continue as the lane becomes a track, PUBLIC BRIDLEWAY. Walk uphill. Turn right, PUBLIC FOOTPATH, at a wooden gate.

Continue ahead, SAUNTON, at the next footpath junction, following an enclosed path to an open field. Continue diagonally right uphill, SAUNTON. Enjoy the view of Croyde and Baggy Point.

The Rock Inn, Georgeham   01271 890322
In Henry Williamson's writings the 17th century Rock features as the 'Higher House'. Both pubs, the Rock and the Lower House, have collections of period photographs: some in the Rock show Williamson in the pub. The author lived in Georgeham between the World Wars and wrote some of his best known books here, including *Tarka the Otter* and *Salar the Salmon*.

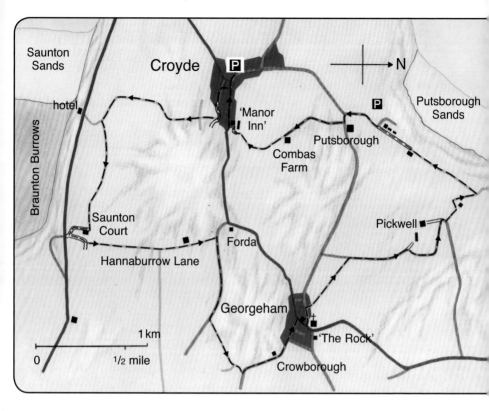

Walk ahead, SAUNTON, over the crest of the hill for another splendid view – Braunton Burrows and Saunton Sands with the Taw/Torridge estuary in the background.

Take the SAUNTON path diagonally left and downhill to a junction. Keep left, SAUNTON COURT. Walk through two fields and follow the track gently downhill, passing to the right of Saunton Court, a late medieval manor house remodelled by Lutyens in 1932.

The track forks. Turn sharp left, PUBLIC BRIDLEWAY. Initially tarred, Hannaburrow Lane becomes a grassy path, rich in wild flowers. (In 1675, this was mapped as one of England's main roads, leading from Ilfracombe to Bideford via a ferry. Devon had no wheeled vehicles in those days, only pack horses.) Continue uphill to the crest, then downhill signed FORDA.

Descend to a tarmac lane and turn right. Bear left after 550 m, PUBLIC FOOTPATH. This leads across a field, over a stile and into an enclosed path. Keep left when the path divides. Turn left onto the lane and continue to a T-junction by the village shop. Turn right, then left at the

14

Lower House – or continue up the lane and take the first right to visit the Rock Inn and then retrace your steps.

Walk downhill past the church. 'Crowberry', one of the cottages on the right, bears a blue plaque as Williamson's sometime home. After a further 50 m, turn right up a footpath, which follows an enclosed track then turns left through a series of well-signed fields and gates.

Turn right at the lane. Follow the lane when it diverts around Pickwell Manor Farm to Pickwell Cross. Follow the lane right, then only 25 m ahead turn left, PUBLIC FOOTPATH. At the next waymark bear left and downhill, but after 50 m turn right, PUBLIC FOOTPATH. This dogleg avoids passing in front of a wooden house. The footpath leads gently downhill to a gate, then more steeply to a second gate.

Turn left onto a well-beaten path – the Coast Path. Follow the Coast Path acorn signs and ignore side-turnings. On reaching the lane, continue ahead, COAST PATH. However, do not take the next Coast Path turning. Continue on the tarmac lane. Don't take the lane for Croyde, but walk ahead, PUTSBOROUGH GEORGEHAM.

Turn right at the pond by Putsborough Manor. At Combas Farm continue ahead PUBLIC BYWAY. Reaching Croyde, follow the lane to the right, then turn right past the front of the Manor Inn (which has another good collection of local period photographs) and follow the lane (which can be quite busy so take care) to the start.

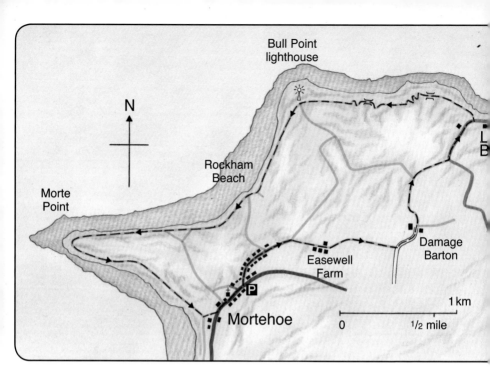

Walk 5   Mortehoe

Distance: 9.5 km (6 miles)
Time: 3 1/4 hours
*Character: This moderately challenging coastal walk has a number
of steep ascents amply compensated for by magnificent views and
dramatic cliff formations, especially at Morte Point.*

From Mortehoe car park, cross the main road into North Morte Road,
signed LIGHTHOUSE LEE. After 500 m, at the end of the road, take
FOOTPATH TO LEE. Walk past caravans to a signpost. Continue ahead,
FOOTPATH TO LEE, with first the washrooms then the shop on your
right, then bear slightly left, FOOTPATH TO LEE, past a house.

Cross a stile and a small field, and bear right up a track. The footpath
continues up a well made enclosed path, then a field edge. At a tarmac track, turn left and follow it down to Damage Barton. Continue
past the front of the farmhouse, turn right and immediately left on a
footpath – in effect continuing in the same direction. A small wooden
board indicates LEE AND BULL POINT.

At the next path junction turn right, FOOTPATH TO LEE. Cross a stile
and continue downhill to another stile and an enclosed path. Turn left

16

on reaching a tarmac lane. Follow it downhill to a 20 mph speed limit sign. Turn left, NATIONAL TRUST DAMAGE CLIFFS, at a small gate and a flight of steps. (You might want to take a look at Lee Bay, an attractive cove, which has an equally attractive pub, the Grampus, inland up a footpath.)

Walk ahead, following Coast Path signs. The Coast Path is well defined and signed all the way to Morte Point and beyond, so the navigation is simple but the walking quite strenuous. The steepest parts are relieved by steps and zig-zags. There are several signed paths back to Mortehoe.

Unless you want to take a short cut, continue ahead, MORTE POINT, a dramatic saw-toothed slate formation. From the Point, follow the Coast Path for another 1.4 km (1500 yards) to a path junction almost beneath some buildings. Bear left uphill, MORTEHOE. When the footpath meets the lane, turn left and continue uphill into Mortehoe where there is a good choice of refreshments.

The lane leads past the 16th century stone and cob Chichester Arms, which has some fine sea pictures, and on past the church. On the left just beyond the church is the Ship Aground. Follow the road round to the right back to the car park.

At the back of the car park is the Mortehoe Heritage Centre, which offers a cameo of local history, in which shipwrecks, farming and tourism all feature. There are also interactive games for children.

Morte Point and the Bull Point Lighthouse

The lighthouse was built in 1879 and rebuilt in 1974, following a cliff fall two years earlier. Its light has a range of 44 km (24 nautical miles). It keeps vessels clear both of Morte Point, where many ships have been wrecked in the past – five in the winter of 1852 alone – and of the Rockham Shoal.

The Ship Aground   01271 870856

The anchor in front of the building belonged to the SS *Collier*, one of the first steamships to carry mail to Australia, which ran aground in 1914. Inside the pub there are period photographs and seascape paintings.

Walk 6 Berrynarbor

Distance: 11km (6³/4 miles)
Time: 3¹/2 hours
Character: This moderately demanding route includes five sharp but fairly short ascents, and much of interest, including some of north Devon's most spectacular coastal views. There is one short section (150m) of narrow verge beside a main road.

Ye Olde Globe 01271 882465

This pub is thought to date from 1675 as an inn, having been converted from a row of three cottages dating from about 1280. It has exposed beams, three stone fireplaces and a collection of antiques, craftsmen's tools and farm implements, as well as period settles. In the pretty beer garden are stocks, capacity one villain.

Hele Mill (limited seasonal opening) is mentioned on a map of 1525, but the present corn mill is of unknown age. Derelict after 1945, it was restored in the 1970s and is run as a museum with a tea garden and various handicrafts.

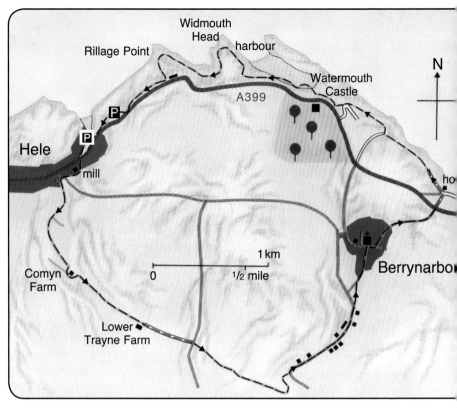

Turn left out of Hele car park. Cross the main road and take the PUBLIC FOOTPATH opposite. This leads through the grounds of Hele Mill. Reaching a tarmac lane, turn right. Follow the lane round the bend and bear left, LITTLETON COMYN TRAYNE. At WITHERIDGE PLACE, turn left up a tarmac track. When the track veers left, continue ahead through a gate, PUBLIC FOOTPATH.

Follow the path (Cat Lane) to Comyn Farm. Turn right then left, PUBLIC BRIDLEWAY. Bear left, through a metal gate, then take the second right as signed, crossing the brook into a muddy enclosed path. (The landowner is considering voluntarily making a drier unofficial route.) Continue ahead from another gate as signed, climbing the field path to another gate. Walk ahead, keeping to the left of the farm, and take the metalled track uphill.

Cross a lane and the high stile opposite. Continue ahead and slightly right to a stile at the lowest point of the field. Walk downhill and slightly right to a stile halfway down the field. Cross the stile and footbridge. Follow the path left and downhill with the stream on your left.

Follow the path on through fields to a lane. Turn left and follow the lane through Sterridge. Bear right onto a short PUBLIC FOOTPATH. Reaching a lane, walk ahead and uphill into Berrynarbor. Opposite the church, turn left to visit Ye Olde Globe Inn, or right to continue the walk.

From the pub, return to the church gate and walk ahead, COMBE MARTIN, following Barton Lane as it curves left and uphill. Continue to the main road. Cross carefully and walk ahead, COAST PATH, to the entrance of Sandy Cove Hotel. Turn left then immediately bear right on OLD COAST ROAD. The road soon becomes a stony track, leading through trees. Just before it joins a tarmac lane, turn right COAST PATH. Follow the beaten path to the right of the campsite, onto a tarmac track then ahead to the busy main road as signed.

Turn right along the pavement, then into an enclosed path. Rejoin the pavement and turn almost immediately right, COAST PATH, opposite Watermouth Castle. Except for an hour either side of some high tides, when walkers must follow the main road for 200m before rejoining the Coast Path at a stile, it is possible to cut across the muddy sand and then turn left up steps, COAST PATH.

Happily, the Coast Path soon diverges from the side of the road. Magnificent views of Watermouth open up, with a series of high cliffs beyond, especially as the path climbs Widmouth Head.

Keep following COAST PATH signs. After Rillage Point the path again runs parallel to the road. At one point you will have to walk on a narrow verge for 150m. Walk through the car park and its picnic area, then rejoin the road, following the pavement downhill to the start.

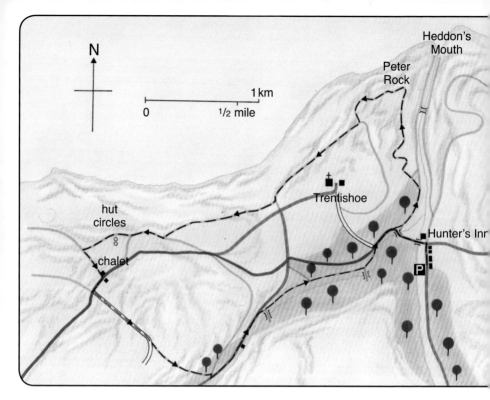

Walk 7   Hunter's Inn and Trentishoe

Distance: 9.7km (6 miles)
Time: 3 hours
Character: A steep climb from Heddon's Mouth Cleave is rewarded with spectacular aerial views of this deep rocky valley and the beach below. The coast path then has dramatic views of steep cliffs. Vertigo sufferers might have a problem, and short stretches of scree demand particular care. The path could be dangerous in high winds. The return route via deep woodland provides a remarkable contrast.

Turn left out of the National Trust car park near Hunter's Inn and walk down the lane to the inn. Take the COMBE MARTIN road. Turn right after 300m, FOOTPATH HEDDON'S MOUTH.

After 450m, turn left COAST PATH COMBE MARTIN. The steep ascent is relieved by zigzags. Take care where there are loose stones (scree). The path levels out towards Peter Rock, a wonderful viewpoint.

Follow the Coast Path west along the high cliffs for 3.6km, ignoring several turnings left. Start thinking about turning inland when the Coast Path passes through a gap in a stone wall.

Immediately beyond this, on the left, there are Bronze Age hut circles, likely to be concealed by bracken in summer. The sloping roof of a chalet then appears on the left. After another 200 m or so, the stony path meets a broad track – there is a short wooden post with an acorn logo at the junction. Turn sharp left and follow the track past the chalet to a tarmac lane.

Turn right and follow the lane for 150 m. Turn left onto a broad track over Holdstone Down, PERMITTED PATH LADIES MILE. After 700 m, diverge left from the track (which curves away to the right) at a short post bearing a white arrow. Follow the grassy path downhill and into a wood. Descend quite steeply to a broader path, and turn sharp right along it.

When you reach a tarmac lane, turn left and follow it for 750 m, then bear right, PUBLIC FOOTPATH HUNTERS INN. Continue ahead on this broad woodland path, following a series of HUNTERS INN signs and ignoring side turnings, until you reach a tarmac lane. Turn right and follow it back to Hunter's Inn and the car park.

Hunter's Inn   01598 763230

Hunter's Inn is decorated with a variety of paintings and local period photographs. Some show the inn before it was burnt down in 1895 – at which time it was thatched.

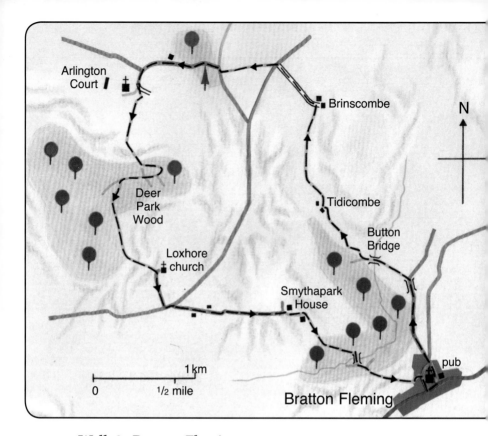

Walk 8   Bratton Fleming

Distance: 11.3km (7 miles)
Time: 3¹/₂ hours
Character: This pleasant walk through fields and woods by quiet footpaths has two steep slopes, but is otherwise gentle. Arlington Court (National Trust), conveniently situated halfway, offers refreshment. It is usually closed on Saturdays – check on the National Trust website or by phoning 01271 850296.

Park carefully on or near Bratton Fleming's Station Road, by the east gate of the church. Walk past the village hall and the school. Keep left, RYE PARK, at Buttonhill Cross. Descend the lane and cross the old railway bridge, with the narrow gauge track of the Lynton & Barnstaple Railway (1898-1935) still *in situ*. Continue for a further 200m then fork left, PUBLIC FOOTPATH, as the lane curves right.

Follow the track down to Button Bridge. Cross, then after 25m turn right through the metal gate and follow the footpath (unsigned at the

time of writing) over wet ground and uphill. Keep left when the path forks and climb steeply.

Follow the footpath signs around Tidicombe Farm, passing to the right of the barn. Turn left and almost immediately right to pass through a small gate. Turn right in front of the farmhouse and continue through the farmyard.

Follow the signed path ahead through fields, paying careful attention to the directional arrows. At Brinscombe Farm, turn left onto the concrete track. Follow it to a lane, cross and continue ahead on PUBLIC BRIDLEWAY. Arriving at a second lane, turn right and follow it as it bends left, then for 800m further. Then turn left (TO PUBLIC BRIDLEWAY), passing a No Through Road sign.

When the lane divides into tracks, keep left for 50m. If you wish to visit Arlington Court, divert right here and return to this point after your visit. Otherwise continue for a further 50m and turn right into a bridleway, DEER PARK WOOD. Turn right at the wooden gate ahead, and left into an enclosed bridleway at the next gate.

Walk on through trees, past a stone obelisk which marks Queen Victoria's Jubilee and down an enclosed path to a stile and a gate.

Follow the track through the gate and downhill until it curves right

to a junction of paths. Continue ahead, LOXHORE CHURCH, then keep left, LOXHORE CHURCH. Emerging from the wood, cut slightly left through the first field to a gate with a blue bridleway sign. Continue along the enclosed path to a lane.

Divert left to visit Loxhore's charming church, otherwise turn right and walk past South Town Farm to a junction. Turn left and then after 60 m right, RIDDLE SMYTHAPARK.

Continue for 1 km. At Smythapark House, turn right, PUBLIC BRIDLEWAY. After 200 m, turn right by an old barn as signed. Continue along the path and downhill into Smythapark Wood. Cross the stream by a footbridge and walk uphill. When the path divides, turn left and uphill. Climb steeply to another path junction. Keep right and uphill, PUBLIC FOOTPATH.

Continue on this path out of the wood. Head up the first field aiming for the top left corner, then straight across a second to a stile. Follow the footpath between houses, turning left then right to a street. Turn right and follow it to the main village street. Turn left and left again into Station Road, and the White Hart.

The White Hart 01598 710977

The inn has a good collection of local period photographs, several showing local characters, and also the building before alterations. Its age is uncertain, but it was recorded as early as 1824, and retains a large stone fireplace. It has an attractive restaurant and beer garden, and offers accommodation.

Walk 9 Swimbridge

Distance: 9.5km (6 miles)
Time: 3 hours
Character: A pleasant pastoral circuit from Swimbridge's historic inn and church. There are no steep ascents, but one very steep descent, which can, however, be avoided. Parts of this walk are likely to be muddy and may be somewhat overgrown – boots and long trousers are recommended.

Start from the parking area in The Square, almost opposite the Jack Russell Inn and by a footbridge leading to the church.

Take the HANNAFORD lane behind the Jack Russell and follow it for 1.2km to Combe Cross. Turn left, BYDOWN DENNINGTON. Continue ahead for only 150m. Turn right over a stile. At the time of writing, the PUBLIC FOOTPATH sign points straight ahead, which is misleading.

The Jack Russell 01271 830366

John (Jack) Russell, the famous hunting parson, was Perpetual Curate of Swimbridge and Landkey from 1833 to 1878. Photographed in full hunting rig and top hat, Russell and his eponymous terriers feature strongly in the inn's well illustrated local history collection, whilst Trump, his original terrier and the progenitor of the breed, is featured on the pub sign.

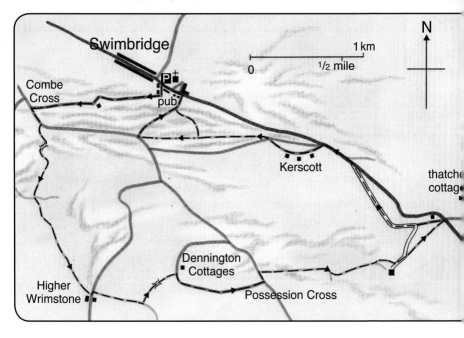

In fact you need to turn left, descend gently and then keep the bottom hedge of the field on your right till you come to a footbridge.

Cross the bridge and follow the signed path through scrub and trees. Cross a stile into a meadow. Continue ahead to the far left corner of the meadow and cross another stile. Do not turn immediately left on the footpath, but turn left on the broader track beyond. Continue on this track to meet a lane at Higher Wrimstone.

Turn left and after only 30 m turn right, PUBLIC FOOTPATH. Go through a metal gate and keep the hedge on your right through a field to a stile. Cross the stile and walk along a grassy track. When the track veers slightly to the right, just before some conifers, turn left at a farm gate and stile with a footpath arrow.

Only 30 m ahead, cross the stile on the right. Cut diagonally left as signed, across the field and down to a footbridge. Continue in the same direction across the next field, aiming slightly to the right of Dennington Cottages.

Cross a stile into a lane and turn right. Follow the lane to Possession Cross. Turn left, SWIMBRIDGE LANDKEY, and after 30 m right over a stile, PUBLIC FOOTPATH. Walk through the field, cross another stile and continue ahead as signed through a series of fields and gates to a concrete stile. Cross and continue ahead with the hedge on your left through the field and into an enclosed path.

When the path forks, keep left and cross a stile, then cross the field to a further stile. Turn left up Tower Farm's concrete track as far as a metal gate on the right. Leave the track and continue ahead as signed across the field, climbing slightly. Cross a stile and walk straight across the field, aiming slightly to the left of the thatched cottages on the horizon. Arriving at a gate, turn left on the tarmac track behind Filleigh Garage and follow the track till it rejoins the Swimbridge road.

Follow the main road for 350 m – beware traffic. Turn left at Kerscott Cross, BYDOWN DENNINGTON HANNAFORD. Divert immediately left and follow the lane through Kerscott and to a lane junction. Bear left and after 50m bear right, PUBLIC BYWAY. Follow the rocky track – until about 1760 the main road from London to Barnstaple! – for 500 m.

You now have a choice between scenic and sedate routes. For the scenic, turn right over a stile, PUBLIC FOOTPATH. A fine view opens up. Follow the footpath ahead for a bird's eye view of Swimbridge. Cut diagonally left across the field, reducing the extreme steepness of the slope, to the bottom left hand corner of the field. Turn right. Follow a stile and steps to a lane, and turn right back into Swimbridge.

For the sedate route, continue along the byway to a junction, then turn right down a narrow lane for SWIMBRIDGE.

Arriving in the village, turn left along the main road to return to the pub and your car.

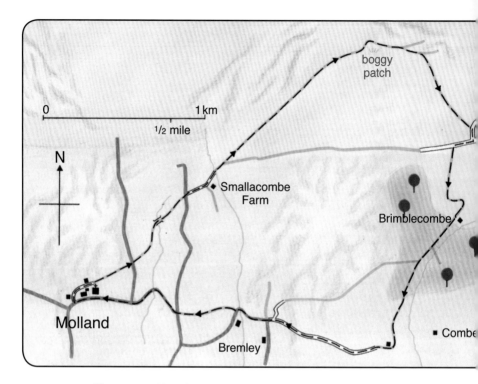

Walk 10 Molland

Distance: 7.7 km (4 3/4 miles)
Time: 2 1/2 hours
*Character: This fairly demanding route includes several steep slopes
but offers magnificent views onto Exmoor. It encompasses typical North
Devon scenery – some open moorland, patchwork fields divided
by high hedgebanks and steep wooded combes sheltering ancient
farmsteads. Molland, a quite unspoilt village, is built around its 15th
century inn and church, noted for its rare unaltered Georgian interior,
the most complete in Devon. Map and compass are recommended for
the open moor.*

Start from the parking area by the church (SS 808284). With your back
to the church turn right and walk past the London Inn. Turn almost
immediately right up a track, soon signed PUBLIC FOOTPATH. Walk
past Bowchurch Farm and uphill, diagonally right across fields as
signed.

Cross a lane and continue into the next field. Follow an old cart
track downhill to a stream. Turn right down steps, over a footbridge

30

and stile. Climb diagonally left, quite steeply, up the field, through a waymarked gate and diagonally right to a lane.

Continue ahead, SMALLACOMBE. The bridleway divides at the farm. Walk ahead into an enclosed track, over a brook and onto the open moor.

When the bridleway divides again, offering two routes to ANSTEY GATE, keep left, up Smallacombe Combe. Continue through the furze on a broadly north-easterly bearing and ignore side tracks. At a five-way path junction, take the second on the right. Keep right when it branches. It circles the top of Anstey's Combe and starts to head in a south-easterly direction.

There are more horse tracks on the ground than are marked on the OS Explorer map, so please check your progress with map and compass. The most obvious horse track leads down to a well surfaced vehicle track. Turn right and follow it downhill to a junction. Turn right. Only 130 m ahead, turn left at a cross-track, clearly signed BRIDLEWAY BREMLEY. Check you have reached this point before continuing.

Follow the bridleway down to a house, Brimblecombe. Turn right as signed. At the first junction of bridleways, continue ahead. At the second junction, bear left on the broad track parallel to the brook.

After 600 m, turn right at the next PUBLIC BRIDLEWAY sign. Walk through Whitley farmyard, out through the automatic gate and on along the tarmac track. At Bremley Cross, walk ahead, MOLLAND.

Follow the lane downhill and over a brook. Turn right up steps and over a stile, PUBLIC FOOTPATH.

Climb directly up the steep but short hill, passing old mine workings on your left, a relic of Exmoor's vanished mineral industry. Cross another stile at the top of the field and walk ahead through fields, keeping the hedge on your right.

Arriving at a tarred lane (Latchgate Cross) walk ahead, MOLLAND. Continue along the lane to the village.

London Inn (01769 550269)

Like the church, the London Inn has a timeless quality and a strong Exmoor flavour. Trophies of the chase and hunting prints adorn the walls; juke boxes and TVs are mercifully absent, but there's a darts board and a skittle alley, whilst euchre completes the triad of pub games that have vanished from many places.